THE SILENT GOODBYE

A JOURNAL FOR COPING WITH LIVING GRIEF

CAMELLE ILONA

For my Family

DEAR KIND SOUL,

First, let me say this: I see you. I know how hard this journey is because I've walk it too. Grieving someone who is still alive can feel like a contradiction—how do you mourn a person who's physically present but no longer fully here? It's a pain that is often silent, misunderstood, and deeply isolating.

When my mum was diagnosed with dementia just after my dad passed away, I found myself grieving not just the life we had, but the life we would never have again. My mum, the vibrant godly woman who raised me, was slowly slipping away before my eyes. I find myself in this strange space, grieving someone who was still with me, yet fading. The weight of that grief was heavy, and it was a loss I never expected.

I created *The Silent Goodbye* because I know how much we need space to process this kind of grief. I need it myself. I need a place where I can be honest about the pain, the confusion, and the unexpected moments of joy. This journal is a space for you to do that. To feel deeply. To release what you're holding onto. To heal at your own pace.

Grieving someone who is still alive is not a straight-forward path. It comes with complex emotions—anger, sadness, guilt, confusion. There may be moments when you're overwhelmed by the loss and others when you wonder if you're allowed to grieve at all. But you are. This is your permission to feel everything. To write about it, cry about it, and let it all out.

I want you to know that as you pour your heart into these pages, you're not alone. There's beauty to be found, even in the heartache. You might not see it yet, but I believe that something beautiful can grow from the pain. I hope this journal can be a guide, a safe place for you to process and release the emotions that come with loving someone who is still here but no longer the same.

Allow yourself to journey through the pain, to reflect on your memories, to confront the reality, and to lean on your faith if that's part of your life. Healing may come slowly, but it will come. And on the other side of this grief, there's a tenderness, a depth, and a strength that you can carry with you for the rest of your life.

Thank you for trusting me with your heart. I'm walking alongside you, even if from afar, and I believe that you will find your way through this. The love you hold for your person is powerful, and this love is worth holding onto, even in the midst of the pain.

With compassion and hope,

Camelle ilona

CONTENTS

INTRODUCTION

GRIEVING SOMEONE WHO IS STILL ALIVE

Grief is often thought of as a response to death, a final separation from someone we love. But grief doesn't always wait for death. Sometimes, we begin grieving when someone is still physically present but emotionally or mentally absent. This type of grief, the kind that lingers in the presence of an illness like dementia or the slow unraveling of a relationship, is profound. It's the pain of watching someone change in ways that make them unrecognizable, yet still loving them deeply.

For me, grieving began long before the final goodbyes. It started when I watched my mother fade away before my eyes. She was diagnosed with Alzheimer's and dementia a week after my father passed away at only 58. It was as though, with his death, we lost a part of her too. The memories that had once tethered us together were slipping from her grasp, and I was left trying to hold on to fragments of the person she once was. It's the strangest feeling, grieving someone who is still alive. They're there, but they're not. You're constantly caught between the person they were and who they're becoming, and it's a tension that is both heartbreaking and surreal.

This journal is for those of you navigating that space —the grief of someone who is still alive. Whether it's because of illness, addiction, or a strained relationship, this type of grief demands a different kind of strength, one that involves balancing the sorrow of loss with the gratitude for what remains. It's a process of grieving the past while trying to stay present, to love them as they are now, even if they are no longer the person they once were.

Through journaling, I found a way to process the emotions that felt too big to carry alone. Writing allowed me to sit with my feelings, to name the anger, the sadness, and even the guilt. I learned that it was okay to feel relief when my mother didn't recognize the weight of her decline, even as I mourned the loss of the woman who raised me. Journaling helped me to navigate the complexities of this type of grief, to find moments of peace amidst the chaos of change, and to honor both my emotions and her legacy.

In these pages, I'll ask you to reflect on your own journey with grief. I'll invite you to remember the person you are grieving and to acknowledge how they have changed. I'll ask you to explore the emotions that arise as you process this slow, painful transition—whether it's anger, sadness, or even moments of joy. Most importantly, I'll encourage you to create space for both the grief and the healing. You may not have control over what's happening to your loved one, but you do have control over how you care for yourself during this process.

This kind of grief is not linear. Some days, you'll feel strong. Other days, the weight of what's happening will knock the wind out of you. That's okay. Grieving someone who is still alive is complex and messy, but it's also an invitation to love more deeply, more consciously, and with more grace. And while the journey may feel long and dark at times, there is beauty on the other side of this process—just as a seed must break and grow underground before it blooms, so too can something beautiful emerge from this grief.

In this journal, I hope you find not only a place to process your emotions but also a companion for the journey. Let these prompts guide you through the stages of grief, from denial and anger to acceptance and healing. As you write, remember that you are not alone in this. There is a community of people, myself included, who understand the pain of grieving someone who is still alive. Together, we can walk through this darkness and find light on the other side. Grieve fully, heal intentionally, and know that beauty can come from even the most difficult seasons of life.

1

REFLECTING ON THE RELATIONSHIP

When someone we love changes before our eyes, it's natural to feel a whirlwind of emotions—sadness, confusion, and even disbelief. This grief can begin while they are still physically present but no longer the person they once were. Today, I invite you to reflect on your relationship with them. Take a moment to sit with your thoughts, a pen in hand, and gently explore the nuances of your connection.

Start by remembering the person they used to be. What were some of the qualities that defined them? Perhaps it was their laugh, their wisdom, or their unwavering support. How did they make you feel when you were together? Write down some of your favourite memories with them—those moments that make you smile even now. These memories are a gift, a reminder that your bond with them remains, even if the present reality feels different.

Next, acknowledge how the relationship has changed. How do you feel when you're with them now? This part may feel painful, but giving voice to these emotions is a step toward healing. Be honest about the sadness, the frustration, or even the guilt that may arise as you reflect. It's okay to mourn the changes while still holding onto the love that remains.

Journaling about your relationship can be a powerful way to honour both who they were and who they are now. It can help you process the loss you feel while also finding new ways to connect with them as they are today. Remember, grief is not just about saying goodbye; it's about finding a new way to say hello.

1. How has my relationship with this person changed over time?

2. What do I miss most about the person they used to be?

3. How do I feel when I'm with them now, compared to before?

4. What are some of my favourite memories with this person?

5. What are the qualities I admire most about them?

6. How have I had to adjust to the changes in our relationship?

7. What is the hardest part about grieving someone who is still alive?

8. In what ways do I still see glimpses of the person they once were?

9. How do I honour who they were, while accepting who they are now?

10. What emotions do I experience when I think about the changes in them?

2

PROCESSING GRIEF

Grief is a heavy, complicated emotion. It comes in waves, sometimes crashing over us when we least expect it. When grieving someone who is still alive, it can feel especially disorienting—how do you mourn someone who is still physically here? Today, I invite you to use your journal as a safe space to process the layers of grief you are experiencing.

Begin by asking yourself, "What does my grief feel like right now?" Is it a quiet sadness, or does it feel more like a sharp pain? Is there a sense of disbelief or numbness? Whatever it is, write it down without judgment. Grief is personal, and there is no right or wrong way to feel.

Consider how your emotions have changed throughout this process. Maybe you've cycled through denial, anger, or acceptance. Maybe you feel a mix of everything. Give yourself permission to feel these emotions fully, even if they are uncomfortable. As you write, try to notice if there's any relief in simply acknowledging your grief.

Journaling can help you externalise the grief that feels too big to carry inside. It's a way to make sense of the senseless and to remind yourself that healing is not about rushing through the pain but learning how to live with it. In these pages, you can process the sadness, frustration, and love that exists within your grief—and in doing so, begin to find peace.

11. What does grief feel like to me right now?

12. How have my emotions changed throughout this process?

13. What does it mean to grieve someone who is still physically present?

14. How do I deal with feelings of anger or frustration related to this person's decline?

15. How can I make space for both grief and gratitude in my heart?

16. What is something I wish I could tell this person?

17. How do I cope with feelings of loss, even though they are still here?

18. What are some ways I can practice self-compassion as I grieve?

19. What does "acceptance" look like for me in this situation?

20. How can I balance the sadness of loss with the joy of the moments we still have together?

3
MEMORIES AND LEGACY

Our memories of those we love can be a source of both comfort and pain. When someone we care about changes or declines, we may find ourselves holding on to the past, cherishing who they used to be. Today, I invite you to use your journal to explore the memories you hold most dear and to reflect on the legacy this person has left in your life.

Start by recalling a specific memory that brings you joy. Maybe it's a shared holiday, a long conversation, or a simple moment of laughter. Write it down in as much detail as you can—what were you wearing, where were you, what did they say? Allow yourself to revisit this memory fully, letting the emotions wash over you. These memories are a reminder of the bond you share, a bond that transcends time and change.

Next, think about the legacy this person has left in your life. What lessons have they taught you? What qualities of theirs do you want to carry forward in your own life? Maybe they were kind, patient, or brave—how can you embody those qualities moving forward?

Journaling about their legacy can help you honour who they were and find ways to keep their spirit alive in your own life. This process is not about holding on to the past but about finding meaning in the memories and continuing to carry them with you, even as life changes.

21. What is one lesson this person has taught me that I will carry with me?

22. What's one thing I'll never forget about them?

23. How can I preserve their legacy in my own life?

24. What are some traditions, habits, or sayings of theirs that I want to pass on?

25. If I could go back in time, what's one thing I would say or do differently with them?

26. How do I want to remember them moving forward?

27. What are some of the qualities they had that I want to embody in my own life?

28. How can I keep their memory alive while they are still with me?

29. What was the last time we had a meaningful conversation? What did it mean to me?

30. How can I honour them in my daily life?

4

FACING THE PRESENT REALITY

One of the most difficult aspects of grieving someone who is still alive is accepting the changes in them. It's a daily process of facing the reality that the person you love is not the same, even though they are still physically here. Today, I invite you to journal about what it feels like to face this present reality and how you are navigating these changes.

Start by asking yourself, "How has my relationship with them changed?" Be honest with your feelings, even if they are difficult to confront. Maybe you feel a sense of loss, frustration, or even confusion. Write about these emotions and how they show up in your daily life. How do you interact with them now compared to before? How does it feel when you're with them?

Next, reflect on how you are coping with these changes. Are there moments when you feel disconnected from them? Are there times when you still feel close? Journaling can help you process the complexity of loving someone who is no longer the same person you once knew.

Facing the present reality doesn't mean letting go of the person they were; it means learning to love them in a new way. This part of the journey may be painful, but it's also an opportunity to find strength, resilience, and grace in the face of change.

31. What are the challenges of seeing them change in front of my eyes?

32. How do I navigate feelings of guilt or regret about our relationship now?

33. How do I cope with the fact that they may not remember important parts of our life together?

34. What's something I need to forgive myself for when it comes to this person?

35. How do I process feelings of loneliness even when they are physically present?

36. What's the hardest part about being with them now?

37. How has this situation affected my daily life?

38. How do I take care of myself while caring for or grieving this person?

39. How can I find moments of peace or joy amid the sadness?

40. What would it look like to fully accept this new reality?

5
FINDING SUPPORT

Grieving someone who is still alive can feel incredibly isolating. Others may not understand the depth of your pain because your loved one is still physically here. Today, I invite you to journal about the support you need during this time and how you can ask for it.

Start by reflecting on who has been there for you during this process. Who do you turn to when you need to talk or when you're feeling overwhelmed? Write about the people who have offered comfort, even if it's just a listening ear. How has their support helped you navigate your grief?

Next, think about what kind of support you need right now. Maybe you need more emotional support, practical help, or simply someone to sit with you in silence. How can you communicate these needs to others? Writing down your thoughts can help you clarify what you need and give you the courage to ask for it.

Journaling about finding support can remind you that you don't have to carry this burden alone. There are people who care about you and want to help, even if they don't fully understand your grief. By reaching out, you allow others to walk alongside you in this journey, offering comfort and care when you need it most.

41. Who can I turn to for support during this time?

42. How can I express my feelings to friends or family members?

43. What do I need most from others during this
time?

44. How do I communicate my emotions to people who may not understand what I'm going through?

45. How can I open myself up to receiving help when I need it?

46. What are some ways I can explain this type of grief to others?

47. How can I ask for space when I need to process my feelings?

48. Who in my life has been a source of comfort during this process?

49. How can I let go of the need to "be strong" for others and prioritise my own healing?

50. What boundaries can I set to protect my emotional well-being?

6

PROCESSING ANGER, GUILT, AND OTHER COMPLEX EMOTIONS

Grief is rarely straightforward. It's a tangled web of emotions—sadness, anger, guilt, and even relief—all mixed together. When grieving someone who is still alive, these emotions can feel even more complicated. Today, I invite you to journal about the complex emotions you are experiencing and how you can begin to process them.

Start by naming the emotions that come up for you. Do you feel angry about the changes in your loved one? Guilty for not being able to do more? Maybe you even feel relief that they aren't fully aware of their decline. Whatever you're feeling, write it down without judgment. These emotions are valid, even if they're uncomfortable.

Next, explore where these emotions are coming from. Why do you feel angry or guilty? What are the thoughts or beliefs driving these feelings? Journaling can help you untangle the complexity of your emotions and begin to make sense of them.

Processing these emotions takes time, and it's okay to not have all the answers right now. Writing about them can be a way to release some of the weight you're carrying and to find a path forward, one step at a time.

51. What do I feel angry about when it comes to this person's situation?

52. How can I release feelings of resentment or guilt?

53. What's something I wish I could change about how I handled this situation?

54. How do I forgive myself for not being able to fix what's happening to them?

55. What are some ways I can express my anger in a healthy way?

56. What do I need to forgive them for, if anything?

57. How can I give myself grace during moments of frustration?

58. What's one small step I can take toward releasing guilt or shame?

59. How do I feel when I think about the future with this person?

60. What's one thing I wish I didn't feel, but do, when I think about them?

7
FAITH AND SPIRITUALITY

For many, faith and spirituality play a crucial role in the grieving process. When someone we love changes or declines, it can challenge our beliefs and force us to wrestle with difficult questions about life, loss, and meaning. Today, I invite you to journal about how your faith or spiritual practice is helping you through this time.

Start by reflecting on how your faith has supported you in the past. What scriptures, prayers, or spiritual teachings bring you comfort? How has your belief in something greater than yourself helped you find peace, even in the midst of pain?

Next, consider how your faith is being challenged. Are there moments when you feel distant from God or question why this is happening? It's okay to have doubts and to bring those doubts to the page. Journaling can be a way to process your questions and to seek answers, even if they aren't clear right now.

Faith can be a source of strength, but it can also be a space where we wrestle with our deepest fears and uncertainties. Writing about your spiritual journey can help you find clarity, hope, and a renewed sense of connection to something greater than the grief you are experiencing.

61. How has my faith or spiritual practice helped me through this grief?

62. What does the Bible or my faith tradition say about grief and loss?

63. How can I find peace in knowing that everything happens in God's time?

64. How has God comforted me through this journey?

65. What role does prayer play in my grieving process?

66. How do I trust God's plan when I don't understand it?

67. How can I use this time to strengthen my faith?

68. What spiritual practices can I turn to for comfort?

69. What are some scriptures or spiritual teachings that bring me hope?

70. How do I reconcile my grief with my faith in God's goodness?

8

LOOKING TOWARD HEALING

Healing from grief is not about forgetting or moving on—it's about learning to live with the loss and finding a new way forward. When grieving someone who is still alive, healing can feel elusive, as the person is still physically present but emotionally or mentally changed. Today, I invite you to journal about what healing might look like for you in this situation.

Begin by asking yourself, "What does healing mean to me?" Is it about finding peace with the changes in your loved one? Is it about letting go of certain expectations? Write about what healing might look like for you, even if it feels far away right now.

Next, reflect on what steps you can take toward healing. Are there small moments of joy or peace that you can cultivate in your daily life? How can you care for yourself as you continue to navigate this grief? Journaling can help you explore the possibilities of healing, even in the midst of ongoing loss.

Healing doesn't mean the grief goes away, but it does mean finding a way to carry it with more ease. Through journaling, you can begin to imagine a future where both the love and the loss coexist, and where you can find moments of beauty and peace amidst the pain.

71. What does healing look like for me in this situation?

72. How can I continue to love and cherish them as they are now?

73. What's one thing I can do today to care for myself emotionally?

74. How can I find peace in the present moment, despite the pain?

75. What's one small joy I've experienced recently, even amid the grief?

76. How can I start to embrace this new chapter of my relationship with them?

77. What are some ways I can cultivate resilience during this time?

78. How do I stay hopeful, even when the future seems uncertain?

79. What would it feel like to let go of the past and accept what is?

80. How do I move forward while still honouring the person I'm grieving?

9
DAILY REFLECTION

Grief can be overwhelming, and it's easy to get lost in the intensity of emotions. One way to navigate this is through daily reflection—a practice of checking in with yourself and your emotions on a regular basis. Today, I invite you to start a daily journaling practice to help you process your grief one day at a time.

Start by asking yourself, "How am I feeling today?" Write down whatever comes to mind, whether it's sadness, anger, or even moments of gratitude. Daily reflection can help you stay connected to your emotions and give you a space to release them.

Next, consider what you need today. Do you need rest, support, or simply a moment of quiet? Journaling about your needs can help you prioritise self-care and ensure that you are taking steps toward healing, even on the hardest days.

Daily journaling doesn't have to be long or complicated. It's simply a way to check in with yourself, to acknowledge your emotions, and to remind yourself that healing is a process that happens one day at a time.

81. What is something I'm grateful for today?

82. What emotion am I feeling most strongly today, and why?

83. What do I need today to feel supported and cared for?

84. How can I create a daily ritual that brings me comfort during this time?

85. What's one thing I can do to nurture myself today?

86. How can I find beauty in the small moments of life?

87. What's one thing that made me smile today, despite the grief?

88. How can I focus on the present moment without worrying about the future?

89. What does my body need right now? Rest? Movement? Nourishment?

90. How can I honour my feelings today, no matter what they are?

10

PROCESSING THE JOURNEY

Grieving someone who is still alive is a long and complex journey. It's filled with ups and downs, moments of clarity, and times of deep confusion. Today, I invite you to reflect on the journey you've been on and to honour the progress you've made, even if it feels small.

Start by looking back on where you were when this process began. How have your emotions shifted over time? What lessons have you learned along the way? Write about the moments that stand out to you, whether they were moments of deep pain or unexpected joy.

Next, consider where you are now. How do you feel about the changes in your loved one and in yourself?

Journaling can help you take stock of the journey and recognise that even though it's been difficult, you've continued to move forward.

Processing the journey is about honouring both the challenges and the growth that comes from grief. Through journaling, you can begin to make sense of this journey and find meaning in the process, even as you continue to walk through it.

91. How have I grown through this process of grieving someone who is still alive?

92. What is one lesson I've learned from this journey so far?

93. How has this experience changed my perspective on life and love?

94. What are some unexpected gifts or insights that have come from this grief?

95. How do I feel about the future, knowing that this person's condition may worsen?

96. How have I found strength in the midst of this pain?

97. What's one way I can honour this person in my daily life, even as they change?

98. How has this experience shaped who I am today?

99. What's something I've discovered about myself through this process?

100. What do I want to carry with me from this journey as I move forward?

ABOUT CAMELLE ILONA FRSA

Camelle ilona FRSA
Author | Speaker & Host
Corporate Journaling Designer

With a passion for enhancing workplace culture and nurturing internal talent, Camelle ilona is dedicated to helping companies thrive through corporate journaling and wellbeing strategies.

Bringing over 15 years of experience from the fashion industry, Camelle previously led the international clergy fashion brand, **House of ilona**. Her journey in fashion culminated in the release of her first book, **Finding Divine Flow**: Seeking, Finding, and Flowing in Purpose—An Entrepreneurial Journey. Since then, she has published numerous titles, primarily journals filled with prompts designed to help individuals dive deep into their thoughts, process their experiences, and express themselves through writing.

In 2019, Camelle took a significant step forward by founding and serving as Editor-in-Chief of **Ordained Magazine**, a platform dedicated to amplifying women's voices in ministry. Under her leadership, she inspired a team of over 100 writers and creatives, fostering a collaborative and empowering environment for storytelling.

Building on her success, Camelle launched **the journaling experience** Podcast & Events, where she spends her time speaking, hosting, facilitating, and writing to guide others in thinking, processing, and flowing through both work and life. With her unique blend of expertise and experience, Camelle is committed to helping individuals and organisations unlock their creative potential.

BOOKING CAMELLE ILONA

Invite Camelle to your organisation/team to
facilitate corporate journaling sessions to think,
process and flow together.

www.Camelleilona.com

ALSO BY CAMELLE ILONA

Living in the Flow Planner 2024 and **90 Day Planners** (available on Amazon). These are GREAT for keeping on track with your goals, for quarterly and for ticking off your daily habits.

Checkout the new Podcast **"the Journaling experience"**
and accompanying journals.

Tactical Today Strategy Tomorrow is a thinking journal for professional growth.

Mother: Beautiful Warrior is 365 journaling prompts for Mom's navigating motherhood while still being true to themselves.

Healing through The Storm is for Journaling Your Way to Peace In the Midst of Mourning.

The Silent Goodbye is a Journal for Coping with Living Grief.

the journaling experience

Podcast & Events

For young professionals and entrepreneurs navigating transition at work and home. It's where we gather weekly to think, process and flow.

Finding Divine Flow is the first book I wrote but this **Journaling Workbook** takes you on a personal journey of Finding Your Divine Flow.

Printed in Great Britain
by Amazon

52067157R00082